I0361345

If you have purchased this Diary without its cover, it may be a stolen book. Neither the publisher nor the author is obligated to provide professional services in any way, legal, health, or in any form related to this book, its contents, advice, or otherwise.

The law and practices vary from country to country and state to state.

If legal or professional information is required, the purchaser or the reader should seek it privately and in a manner best suited to their particular needs and circumstances.

The author and publisher expressly disclaim any liability that may be incurred from the information within this book.

All rights reserved. No part of this book, including the interior design, images, cover design, diagrams, or any intellectual property (IP), icons, and photographs, may be reproduced or transmitted in any form by any means (electronic, photocopying, recording, or otherwise) without the prior permission of the publisher. ©

Copyright© 2023 MSI Australia

All rights reserved.

ISBN: 978-1-7636806-1-6

Published by How2Books
Under licence from MSI Ltd, Australia
Company Registration No: 96963518255
NSW, Australia

See our website: www.how2books.com.au
Or contact by email: sales@how2books.com.au
Covers and Copyright owned by MSI, Australia

MSI acknowledges the author and images, text, and photographs used in this book.

Published by How2Books

10% of the sale of each book helps to support Diabetes Type One and Cancer Research.

The Magic of Chelsea 2025 DIARY

Friends of Chelsea...
Chelsea Pensioners

Thank you, Arthur and Mary; you were lovely to get to know...

JANUARY

1)	Wednesday
2)	Thursday
3)	Friday
4)	Saturday

JANUARY

5)	Sunday
6)	Monday
7)	Tuesday
8)	Wednesday

JANUARY

9)	Thursday
10)	Friday
11)	Saturday
12)	Sunday

JANUARY

13)	Monday
14)	Tuesday
15)	Wednesday
16)	Thursday

JANUARY

17)	Friday

18)	Saturday

19)	Sunday

20)	Monday

JANUARY

21)	Tuesday
22)	Wednesday
23)	Thursday
24)	Friday

JANUARY

25) Saturday

26) Sunday

27) Monday

28) Tuesday

JANUARY

| 29) | Wednesday |
|---|---|//

30)	Thursday

31)	Friday

Your Notes

A Traditional Semi-Curved, Massed-Line Arrangement

With mystical colours, this traditional line, semi-curve arrangement gives joy and peace when studying the design's elegant and artistic characteristics.

FEBRUARY

1)	Saturday
2)	Sunday
3)	Monday
4)	Tuesday

FEBRUARY

5) Wednesday

6) Thursday

7) Friday

8) Saturday

FEBRUARY

9)	Sunday
10)	Monday
11)	Tuesday
12)	Wednesday

FEBRUARY

13) Thursday
14) Friday
15) Saturday
16) Sunday

FEBRUARY

17)	Monday
18)	Tuesday
19)	Wednesday
20)	Thursday

FEBRUARY

21) Friday

22) Saturday

23) Sunday

24) Monday

FEBRUARY

25)	Tuesday
26)	Wednesday
27)	Thursday
28)	Friday

Your Notes

Meconopsis – Rare Blue Poppy...

MARCH

1)	Saturday
2)	Sunday
3)	Monday
4)	Tuesday

MARCH

5)	Wednesday
6)	Thursday
7)	Friday
8)	Saturday

MARCH

9)	Sunday
10)	Monday
11)	Tuesday
12)	Wednesday

MARCH

13) Thursday

14) Friday

15) Saturday

16) Sunday

MARCH

17) Monday

18) Tuesday

19) Wednesday

20) Thursday

MARCH

21)	Friday
22)	Saturday
23)	Sunday
24)	Monday

MARCH

25) Tuesday
26) Wednesday
27) Thursday
28) Friday

MARCH

29)	Saturday
30)	Sunday
31)	Monday

Your Notes

Heavenly Clematis

To see the heavenly blooms and to have the privilege of taking these photographs is indeed a life treasure...

APRIL

1)	Tuesday
2)	Wednesday
3)	Thursday
4)	Friday

APRIL

5) Saturday

6) Sunday

7) Monday

8) Tuesday

APRIL

9)	Wednesday
10)	Thursday
11)	Friday
12)	Saturday

APRIL

13)	Sunday
14)	Monday
15)	Tuesday
16)	Wednesday

APRIL

17) Thursday

18) Friday

19) Saturday

20) Sunday

APRIL

21)	Monday

22)	Tuesday

23)	Wednesday

24)	Thursday

APRIL

25)	Friday

26)	Saturday

27)	Sunday

28)	Monday

APRIL

29)	Tuesday
30)	Wednesday

Your Notes

Not All Boots Are Made for Walking...!

Not all boots are made for walking, especially past the 'Use By Date.' If this is so, use old shoes and boots as planters for growing various mushrooms! This could become a family hobby and give great food rewards.

(Please buy all mushroom packs from reputable suppliers)

MAY

1)	Thursday
2)	Friday
3)	Saturday
4)	Sunday

MAY

5)	Monday
6)	Tuesday
7)	Wednesday
8)	Thursday

MAY

9)	Friday

10)	Saturday

11)	Sunday

12)	Monday

MAY

13)	Tuesday
14)	Wednesday
15)	Thursday
16)	Friday

MAY

17)	Saturday

18)	Sunday

19)	Monday

20)	Tuesday

MAY

21)	Wednesday
22)	Thursday
23)	Friday
24)	Saturday

MAY

25)	Sunday
26)	Monday
27)	Tuesday
28)	Wednesday

MAY

29) Thursday
30) Friday
31) Saturday

Your Notes

Wildflowers in Abundance...

JUNE

1)	Sunday
2)	Monday
3)	Tuesday
4)	Wednesday

JUNE

5)	Thursday
6)	Friday
7)	Saturday
8)	Sunday

JUNE

9)	Monday
10)	Tuesday
11)	Wednesday
12)	Thursday

JUNE

13)	Friday
14)	Saturday
15)	Sunday
16)	Monday

JUNE

17)	Tuesday
18)	Wednesday
19)	Thursday
20)	Friday

JUNE

21)	Saturday
22)	Sunday
23)	Monday
24)	Tuesday

JUNE

25)	Wednesday
26)	Thursday
27)	Friday
28)	Saturday

JUNE

29)	Sunday
30)	Monday

Your Notes

Part of The Fun of The Day...

A Rikshaw for hire.... The perfect transport to get to the Chelsea Flower Show...

JULY

1)	Tuesday
2)	Wednesday
3)	Thursday
4)	Friday

JULY

5)	Saturday
6)	Sunday
7)	Monday
8)	Tuesday

JULY

9) Wednesday

10) Thursday

11) Friday

12) Saturday

JULY

13)	Sunday

14)	Monday

15)	Tuesday

16)	Wednesday

JULY

17) Thursday
18) Friday
19) Saturday
20) Sunday

JULY

21)	Monday

22)	Tuesday

23)	Wednesday

24)	Thursday

JULY

25) Friday

26) Saturday

27) Sunday

28) Monday

JULY

29)	Tuesday
30)	Wednesday
31)	Thursday

Your Notes

Combinations of Vegetable & Flower Plantings

AUGUST

1)	Friday	
2)	Saturday	
3)	Sunday	
4)	Monday	

AUGUST

5)	Tuesday

6)	Wednesday

7)	Thursday

8)	Friday

AUGUST

9) Saturday

10) Sunday

11) Monday

12) Tuesday

AUGUST

13)	Wednesday
14)	Thursday
15)	Friday
16)	Saturday

AUGUST

17) Sunday

18) Monday

19) Tuesday

20) Wednesday

AUGUST

21) Thursday

22) Friday

23) Saturday

24) Sunday

AUGUST

25)	Monday

26)	Tuesday

27)	Wednesday

28)	Thursday

AUGUST

29)	Friday
30)	Saturday
31)	Sunday

Your Notes

Living Art Forms...

Once we work with space, as in the above designs, volume is created. In the above, clever thinking has made a little look a lot...!

SEPTEMBER

1)	Monday
2)	Tuesday
3)	Wednesday
4)	Thursday

SEPTEMBER

5)	Friday
6)	Saturday
7)	Sunday
8)	Monday

SEPTEMBER

9)	Tuesday

10)	Wednesday

11)	Thursday

12)	Friday

SEPTEMBER

13)	Saturday
14)	Sunday
15)	Monday
16)	Tuesday

SEPTEMBER

17)	Wednesday
18)	Thursday
19)	Friday
20)	Saturday

SEPTEMBER

21)	Sunday

22)	Monday

23)	Tuesday

24)	Wednesday

SEPTEMBER

25) Thursday

26) Friday

27) Saturday

28) Sunday

SEPTEMBER

29) Monday

30) Tuesday

Your Notes

A ROPE TUNNEL – A DIFFERENT EXPERIENCE...

There are many different experiences when one visits the Chelsea Flower Show; walking through a rope-lined tunnel with beautiful flowers was new and exciting...

OCTOBER

1)	Wednesday
2)	Thursday
3)	Friday
4)	Saturday

OCTOBER

5)	Sunday

6)	Monday

7)	Tuesday

8)	Wednesday

OCTOBER

9)	Thursday

10)	Friday

11)	Saturday

12)	Sunday

OCTOBER

13)	Monday
14)	Tuesday
15)	Wednesday
16)	Thursday

OCTOBER

17)	Friday
18)	Saturday
19)	Sunday
20)	Monday

OCTOBER

21)	Tuesday
22)	Wednesday
23)	Thursday
24)	Friday

OCTOBER

25)	Saturday

26)	Sunday

27)	Monday

28)	Tuesday

OCTOBER

29)	Wednesday
30)	Thursday
31)	Friday

Your Notes

A New Approach in Flower Designs

With our rising consciousness of protecting the planet, floral artists are looking at ways to love what they do while also being mindful of sustainability. Rope is a sustainable product and was used at the Show in a variety of different ways; above is just one...!

NOVEMBER

1)	Saturday
2)	Sunday
3)	Monday
4)	Tuesday

NOVEMBER

5)	Wednesday
6)	Thursday
7)	Friday
8)	Saturday

NOVEMBER

9)	Sunday

10)	Monday

11)	Tuesday

12)	Wednesday

NOVEMBER

13)	Thursday
14)	Friday
15)	Saturday
16)	Sunday

NOVEMBER

17) Monday
18) Tuesday
19) Wednesday
20) Thursday

NOVEMBER

21)	Friday
22)	Saturday
23)	Sunday
24)	Monday

NOVEMBER

25)	Tuesday
26)	Wednesday
27)	Thursday
28)	Friday

NOVEMBER

29)	Saturday
30)	Sunday

Your Notes

A Tribute to The Chelsea Pensioners...

The Harkness Rose now attributed to the Chelsea Pensioners and such a fitting gesture to such a wonderful organisation.

DECEMBER

1)	Monday
2)	Tuesday
3)	Wednesday
4)	Thursday

DECEMBER

5)	Friday
6)	Saturday
7)	Sunday
8)	Monday

DECEMBER

| 9) Tuesday |
| 10) Wednesday |
| 11) Thursday |
| 12) Friday |

DECEMBER

13)	Saturday
14)	Sunday
15)	Monday
16)	Tuesday

DECEMBER

17)	Wednesday

18)	Thursday

19)	Friday

20)	Saturday

DECEMBER

21)	Sunday

22)	Monday

23)	Tuesday

24)	Wednesday

DECEMBER

25)	Thursday

26)	Friday

27)	Saturday

28)	Sunday

DECEMBER

29)	Monday
30)	Tuesday
31)	Wednesday

Your Notes

Flowers to Make Your Heart Sing...

www.ingramcontent.com/pod-product-compliance
Lightning Source LLC
Chambersburg PA
CBHW061738070526
44585CB00024B/2726